FOOTBALL

ROBBIE BYERLY

We want the ball for football.

We want the helmet for football.

We want the shoes for football.

We want the pads for football.

We want the shirts for football.

We want the players for football.

We want the lines for football.

We want the field for football.

We want the seats for football.

We want the goal for football.

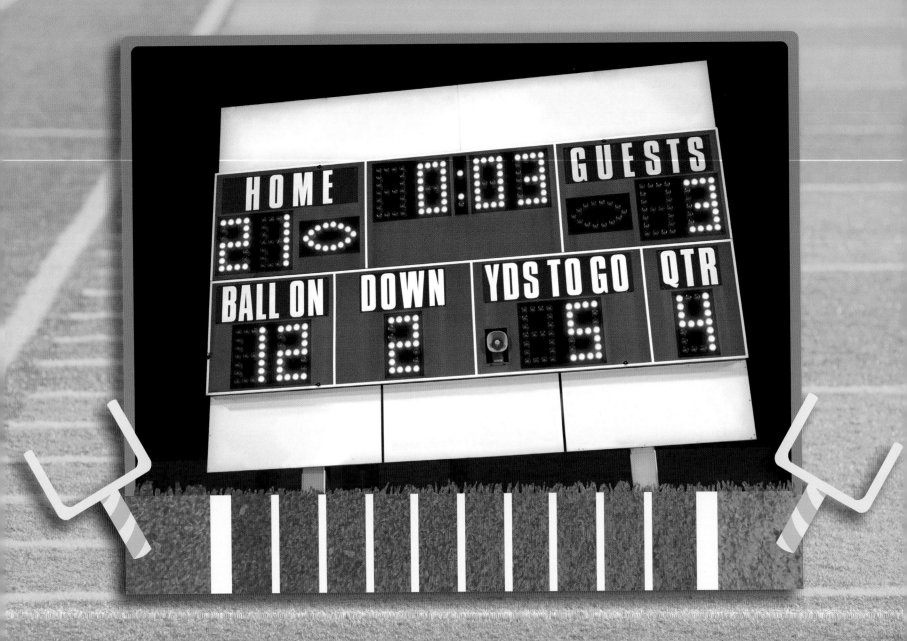

We want the scoreboard for football.

We want the people for football.

We want the trophy for football.

We want the bus for football.

POWER WORDS

How many can you read?

We

we

want

the

for